CREATIVE COMPANIES

THE STORY OF COCA COLA

AF653833

VALERIE BODDEN

JAICO PUBLISHING HOUSE

Ahmedabad Bangalore Chennai
Delhi Hyderabad Kolkata Mumbai

Published by Jaico Publishing House
A-2 Jash Chambers, 7-A Sir Phirozshah Mehta Road
Fort, Mumbai - 400 001
jaicopub@jaicobooks.com
www.jaicobooks.com

Published in arrangement with
The Creative Company
123 South Broad Street, Mankato, MN 56001, USA

To be sold only in India, Bangladesh, Bhutan,
Pakistan, Nepal, Sri Lanka and the Maldives.

Design and Production by Zeno Design

Photographs by Alamy (Steve Cavalier, Ian Dagnall, Joan Gamell Farré , Peter Horree, INTERFOTO Pressebildagentur, Andre Jenny, Tom Mackie, Jenny Matthews, The Natural History Museum, Walter Pietsch), ASSOCIATED PRESS, Corbis (Bettmann, Kevin Fleming, Josh Westrich/zefa), Getty Images (Blank Archives, Margaret Bourke-White//Time Life Pictures, Hulton Archive, Rod Long, George Marks, M&C Saatchi Sport & Entertainment, Justin Sullivan)

Copyright © 2009 Creative Education

Coca-Cola® and the products discussed in this book are either trademarks or registered trademarks of The Coca-Cola Company. Trademarks associated with products of other companies mentioned are the trademarks of their respective owners. This is not an official publication of The Coca-Cola Company, and the views set out herein are solely those of the author.

THE STORY OF COCA COLA
ISBN 978-81-8495-773-0

First Jaico Impression: 2015
Eighth Jaico Impression: 2025

No part of this book may be reproduced or utilized in any form or by any means, electronic or mechanical including photocopying, recording or by any information storage and retrieval system, without permission in writing from the publishers.

Page design and layout: Special Effects, Mumbai

Printed by
Trinity Academy For Corporate Training Limited, Mumbai

CREATIVE COMPANIES

THE STORY OF COCA-COLA

Cola

Every second of every day, people everywhere—13,000 of them—pop open a Coca-Cola product. That adds up to more than one billion Coca-Cola products being consumed every day! With people in nearly 200 countries downing Coca-Cola, it's no wonder the soft drink has become the world's most valuable brand—and the most recognized product on the planet. Relying on clever advertising, catchy slogans, and a connection with people around the world, the Coca-Cola Company today earns $24 billion a year selling nearly 2,400 different products, including soft drinks, juices, teas, sports drinks, and bottled water. Yet, the world's largest nonalcoholic beverage producer is still known best for its namesake and the product that got it all started more than a century ago: Coca-Cola.

1
Discovering Coca-Cola

When John Pemberton, a pharmacist from Atlanta, Georgia, began to mix together the ingredients that would later become Coca-Cola, his intention was not to create a soft drink at all but a tonic for headaches. Working in the back of his shop in 1886, Pemberton mixed fruit syrup, extracts of the cola nut and the coca leaf, and other ingredients in a three-legged brass pot, stirring and heating them until they formed a sticky brown syrup.

After sampling his tonic, Pemberton decided to take it to Jacobs' Pharmacy, the largest drugstore in Atlanta, where the manager agreed to mix it with water and sell it at his soda fountain for five cents a glass.

Before the new drink could be promoted, however, it needed a name, and Pemberton's business partner, Frank Robinson, suggested "Coca-Cola," because he thought the two Cs would look good in advertisements. He carefully penned the beverage's name in flowing script—the same that is used today—and the partners placed their first ad for the beverage in The Atlanta Journal, proclaiming that Coca-Cola was "Delicious! Refreshing! Exhilarating! Invigorating!"

As Jacobs' Pharmacy continued to sell Coca-Cola, someone added carbonated water to the drink in place of plain water (whether intentionally or not, no one knows), and customers who tried the new bubbly drink liked it even better. Soon, Coca-Cola was being sold as a carbonated beverage in soda fountains around Atlanta. In addition to continued advertising in the form of hand-painted Coca-Cola signs at drugstores, Pemberton and Robinson began to issue coupons for free samples of the drink as a way to get customers to try the beverage. Although many liked the new cola beverage, sales during the first year were slow, bringing the partners only $50, which didn't even cover the $75 in expenses they had racked up.

Soon, Pemberton's health began to deteriorate, and he decided to sell shares of his business to his partners. In 1888, shortly before he died, Pemberton sold his last remaining share to an Atlanta doctor and pharmacist named Asa G. Candler. By 1891, Candler had bought out the other people who owned shares of the business, spending a total of $2,300, and he formed the Coca-Cola Company the next year.

Because soda fountain operators often complained that the original formula for Coca-Cola spoiled, Candler quickly set out to change the syrup. In addition to improving the product, Candler also put a heavy emphasis on promoting

Many early Coca-Cola advertisements aimed to create an image that was both classy and casual it. Besides continuing Pemberton's tradition of distributing free drink coupons, he created banners, calendars, serving trays, posters, clocks, paper fans, and other items, all bearing the Coca-Cola name.

As a result of Candler's marketing focus, sales of Coca-Cola rose quickly, reaching nearly 50,000 gallons (189,270 l) a year by 1893, up from Pemberton's 25 gallons (95 l) in 1886. With such a huge increase in sales, the Coca-Cola Company began to expand, opening syrup manufacturing plants in Dallas, Texas, in 1894 and in Chicago, Illinois, and Los Angeles, California, in 1895. By then, Coca-Cola was being sold in every state and territory of the United States.

Despite Coca-Cola's widespread popularity, people could buy the

Soda fountains, popular gathering places in the early 1900s, drove much of Coca-Cola's early success product only at soda fountains; there was no way for them to bring it home. Then, in 1894, a Mississippi soda fountain operator named Joseph Biedenharn set up a bottling machine in his store, becoming the first person to bottle the drink. When Biedenharn sent a case of the bottled soft drink to Candler, Candler pronounced it "fine" but took no further action.

Then, in 1899, Candler was again approached with the idea of bottling Coca-Cola when two lawyers from Tennessee, Benjamin Thomas and Joseph Whitehead, asked him for exclusive rights to bottle and sell the beverage. Candler granted their request, and the two men soon joined with John Lupton, another Tennessee lawyer, and began to set up their bottling operation. Because there was no way for the three men to bottle enough Coca-Cola to supply the whole country themselves, they sold bottling rights to independent bottlers. Within 10 years, nearly 400 plants were bottling Coca-Cola; that number soon increased to 1,000. Throughout the early 1900s,

> *"Coca-Cola is … a sublimated essence of all that America stands for, a decent thing, honestly made."*
>
> William Allen White,
> Newspaper Editor

The tropical coca plant is the source of both an important Coca-Cola ingredient and the drug cocaine

SPICED HOT
CIDER
HOT
CHOCOLATE
25¢
FRESH
LEMONADE

The Soda Fountain

Beginning in the early 1800s, soda fountains could be found in drugstores across America. In many small towns, soda fountains were gathering places, where people could socialize while enjoying a cool beverage or light snack such as a sandwich or ice cream sundae. Early soda fountain flavors included orange, lemon, sarsaparilla, berry, ginger ale, and root beer. As with Coca-Cola, the drinks were made of flavored syrup mixed with carbonated water. After they ordered their drink, customers could mingle at the soda fountain's bar or enjoy their own private table, sometimes surrounded by tall plants that afforded extra privacy. Many soda fountains were luxuriously decorated, with marble countertops, tile floors, and high ceilings. The actual fountains, or syrup dispensers, were also ornate structures, some reaching more than five feet (1.5 m) high. Many were adorned with elaborately carved animals, and their marble bases were surrounded by spigots to dispense the syrup.

bottling plants were even established outside the U.S., in such places as Cuba, Panama, Canada, and Puerto Rico.

Even as it was expanding, though, the Coca-Cola Company was also dealing with some troubling issues, as people began to claim that Coca-Cola's use of the coca leaf meant that it contained cocaine. In 1901, Candler issued a pamphlet revealing that a study had found only a trace amount of cocaine in the syrup, an amount "so small that it would be simply impossible for anyone to form the cocaine habit from drinking Coca-Cola." Still, soon after releasing the pamphlet, Candler charged a chemist with the task of removing the cocaine from the syrup, which was accomplished by 1905.

Despite the negative publicity surrounding the presence of cocaine in the drink, sales continued to climb, fueled by a huge advertising budget that made Coke (as the product was often called) the best advertised item in America. In 1904, the company sold a record one million gallons (3.8 million l); by 1910, it was selling more than four million gallons (15 million l) a year. Coca-Cola was well on its way to becoming the world's soft drink.

2
Worldwide Growth

Because of its great success, Coca-Cola soon found the market flooded with hundreds of imitation soft drinks, including King Cola, Cola Ree, Cold Cola, Koca-Nola, and Ko-Kola. In order to defend its trademarked product, the company began to sue such imitators in 1906.

One case in particular, against the Koke Company of America, dragged on for years and was taken all the way to the U.S. Supreme Court, which declared in 1920 that Coca-Cola was "a single thing coming from a single source, and well known to the community," and that Koke was a fraud and could no longer be sold under the sound-alike name.

As it battled imitators, the Coca-Cola Company also found a unique way to make its product stand out from the others. In 1916, the company began using a new bottle. Instead of the straight sides found on all other soft drink bottles, the new Coca-Cola bottle featured contoured sides, making it recognizable by feel alone. The design was so unique, in fact, that 60 years later, the U.S. Patent Office granted it trademark status, making it one of the few packages ever to be trademarked.

Despite Coca-Cola's continuing success, Asa Candler decided in 1916 to leave the company to serve as Atlanta's mayor. In his place, his son Charles Howard Candler assumed leadership of the company. A year later, in October 1917,

Coca-Cola found itself facing a near-crisis, as the U.S. government, which had entered World War I in April, declared that sugar would be rationed. Since sugar was one of the main ingredients in its product, the Coca-Cola Company was hit hard. "We are finding it exceedingly difficult to secure sufficient amounts of sugar and other material to keep our plants running, and even where we are able to obtain raw materials, it is at such prices that practically eliminate all profits," Sam Dobbs, the company's vice president and manager of sales and advertising, wrote to one of his salesmen. Although the sugar shortage put many soft drink companies out of business, Coca-Cola survived, and when sugar restrictions were removed in 1919, sales of the product boomed.

The year 1919 also saw new ownership of the Coca-Cola Company when a group of investors led by Atlanta banker Ernest Woodruff bought it for $25 million. Woodruff and his partners immediately offered stock in the company to the public. Although the stock sold quickly, Coca-Cola

Coca-Cola's swoopy lettering and unique bottle design helped separate it from its many imitators was soon facing trouble again. Following the sugar rationing of World War I, sugar prices began to rise steeply, reaching 28 cents a pound (.45 kg) in 1920. Fearing that prices would continue to skyrocket, Charles Howard Candler (who continued to serve as chairman) made a deal with sugar suppliers to purchase six months' worth of sugar for 28 cents a pound. Then, shortly after the deal was made, sugar prices fell dramatically to 10 cents a pound. The Coca-Cola Company was now stuck with huge amounts of overpriced sugar. Sparked by this crisis, Coca-Cola soon created a new ad campaign, with the slogan "Thirst Knows No Season," in an attempt to get people to consume their soft drink—which was typically considered a summer refreshment—year-round. The campaign worked, and soon the overpriced sugar was gone.

In April 1923, the Coca-Cola Company again faced change as Woodruff's son Robert Winship Woodruff was elected president. He quickly instituted a new quality training program to establish standards for selling Coca-Cola at soda

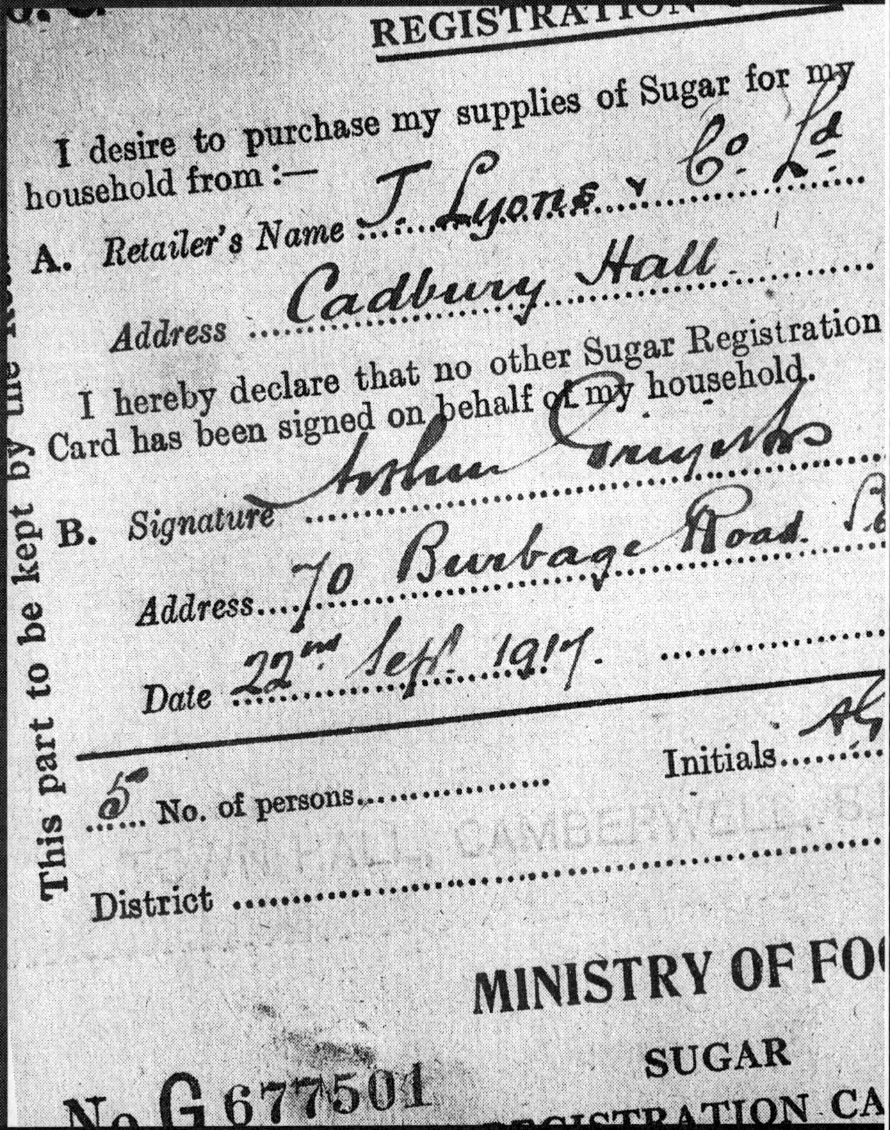

REGISTRATION

I desire to purchase my supplies of Sugar for my household from :—

A. *Retailer's Name* J. Lyons & Co. Ltd

Address Cadbury Hall

I hereby declare that no other Sugar Registration Card has been signed on behalf of my household.

B. *Signature* [illegible]

Address 70 Burbage Road

Date 22nd Sept. 1917

Initials

5 No. of persons

District

MINISTRY OF FO

SUGAR

No G 677501

This part to be kept by the

Sugar rationing during the World War I years was closely monitored, limiting Coca-Cola's production fountains and in bottles, ensuring that no matter where—or in what form—a customer purchased a Coca-Cola, it would always taste the same.

In addition to guaranteeing the quality of Coca-Cola, Woodruff also wanted to make the product easier to purchase. In 1923, the company introduced the six-bottle carton, meaning that consumers now had the option of purchasing something besides single bottles or heavy wooden crates of the soft drink. In the late 1920s, Coca-Cola also introduced its first vending machine, consisting of a chest of ice filled with Coke. Although this model still required customers to pay a clerk before taking a Coke, in the early 1930s, coin-operated vending machines began to appear.

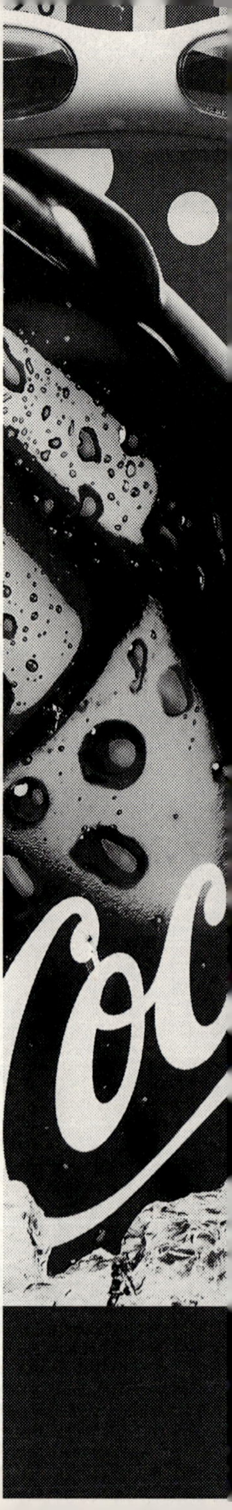

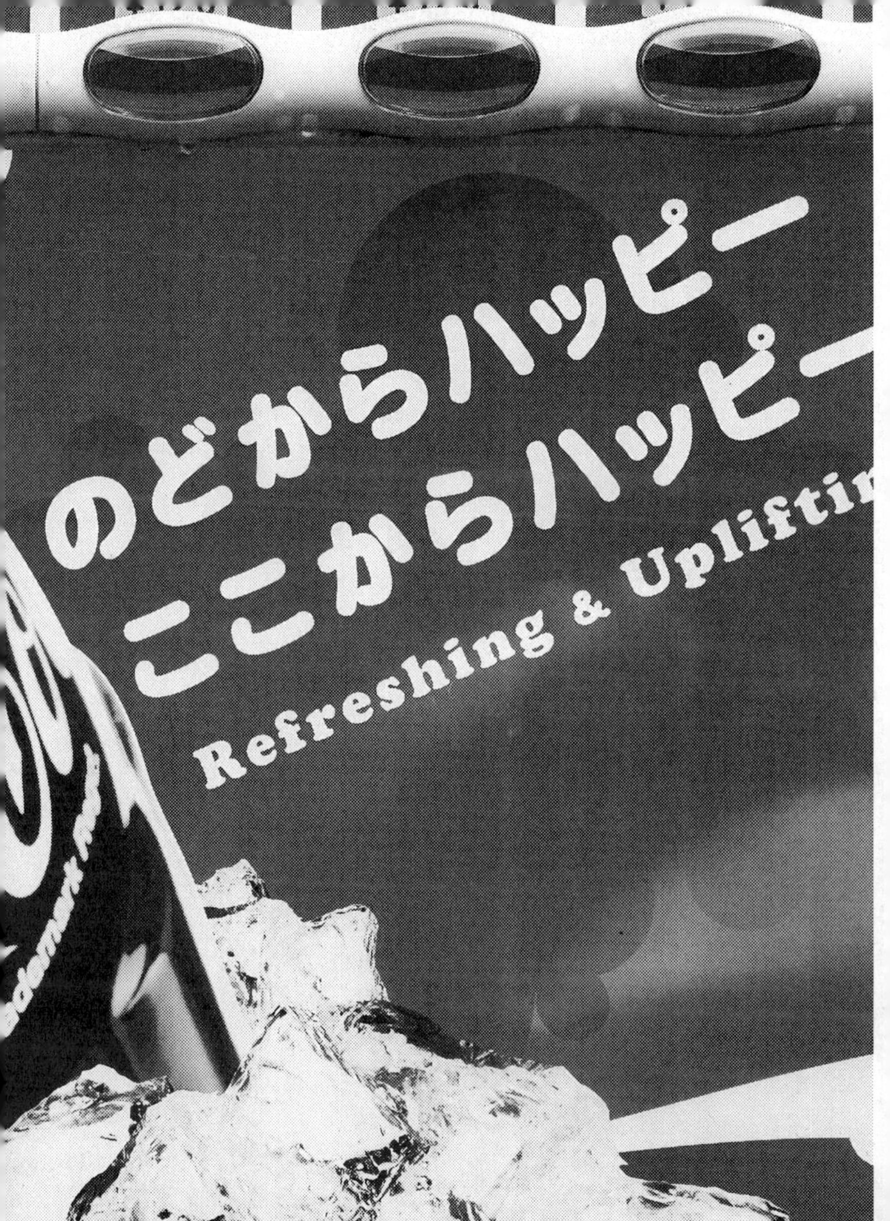

Vending machines, simplistic and rare in the 1930s, are today found by the millions throughout the world

Thirst asks nothing more
Pause... Go refreshed
Coca-Cola
5¢
way
a tired
ty face"
Me too!
"Thirst asks nothing mor
Coca-Cola
ICE COLD
Coca-Cola
DRINK
Coca-Col
Season's Greetings
Coca-Cola

Santa's New Look

As unlikely as it may seem, Coca-Cola's advertisements have influenced not only how people think of the soft drink but also how they think of Santa Claus. In 1931, Coca-Cola decided to use the image of Santa Claus in its holiday ad campaign. The only problem was that, at that time, there were many different images of Santa Claus. Some pictured him as a jolly elf; others portrayed him as tall and thin. In order to solve this problem, the Coca-Cola Company hired artist Haddon Sundblom to paint a new Santa for its ads. The Santa he created was chubby and cheerful, with a white beard and round, red cheeks—and, of course, he enjoyed Coca-Cola. Today, Sundblom's image of Santa (with or without the Coke) is the one that comes to mind when most people think about jolly old St. Nick.

Even as these innovations began to boost sales of Coca-Cola in the U.S., the company set in motion a structured program to distribute Coke around the world. In 1920, a company in France became the first European bottler of Coca-Cola, and in 1926, Woodruff created the Foreign Department (which later became the Coca-Cola Export Corporation) to continue Coca-Cola's spread across the globe. In 1928, Coca-Cola was introduced to people from around the world when it was served at the Olympic Games in Amsterdam.

Part of the reason for the Coca-Cola Company's continued expansion during these years was once again its focus on advertising, as Woodruff sought to make Coca-Cola a part of everyone's daily life. By sponsoring radio programs, painting its name on walls and billboards, and splashing its ads across newspaper and magazine pages, Coca-Cola was able to lay claim to two-thirds of the American drink market, as well as a growing share of the market in other parts of the world. Even during the Great Depression, Coca-Cola sales remained fairly strong, as people could always find a nickel for a Coke.

3

Going to War

On December 7, 1941, the Japanese bombed the U.S. naval base at Pearl Harbor, Hawaii, drawing America into World War II. By that time, Coca-Cola was being bottled in 44 countries, many of them U.S. allies and some of them—such as Germany—U.S. enemies. With America's entry into the war, Robert Woodruff ordered the company "to see that every man in uniform gets a bottle of Coca-Cola for five cents, wherever he is and whatever it costs the company."

Even as the company was gearing up to fulfill Woodruff's directive, in 1943 a message arrived from General Dwight Eisenhower, the commander of the Allied forces in Europe. Eisenhower requested that the company send the materials needed for 10 bottling plants, along with three million filled bottles of Coke. Eisenhower's request was quickly granted, and soon Coca-Cola bottling plants were set up close to Allied forces throughout Europe and the Pacific; some of the plants were even portable and followed the advancing armies. "Technical Observers" from the company delivered Coke to the soldiers, sometimes facing great danger—three were killed during the course of the war. By the end of hostilities, the company had established 64 new bottling plants overseas.

For the grateful soldiers who received the bottled Coca-Cola, the drink wasn't only a way to quench their thirst; it was a reminder of home. As private Dave Edwards wrote to his brother from Italy in 1944, "Today was such a big day that I had to write and tell you about it. Everyone in the company got a Coca-Cola. That might not seem like much to you, but I wish you could see some of these guys who have been overseas for 20 months. They clutch their Coke to their chest, run to their tent and just look at it. No one has drunk theirs yet, for after you drink it, it's gone; so they don't know what to do." With soldiers clamoring for Coca-Cola, more than five billion bottles of the drink were served to military personnel during the war.

Besides providing a taste of home for American soldiers, the new Coca-Cola bottling plants set up during the war introduced local people to the product, opening new markets for growth when the war ended in 1945. Many of the company's wartime bottling plants were converted to peacetime use after the war, and by the early 1950s, more than 25 percent of Coca-Cola's sales came from overseas. In May 1950, *Time* magazine acknowledged Coca-Cola's worldwide success with a cover story entitled "World and Friend." The cover of the magazine featured an image of a red

During World War II, Coca-Cola was a treasured taste of home for U.S. soldiers on the battle lines

Coca-Cola disk serving a bottle of Coke to a happy globe, and the text of the article applauded Coca-Cola's efforts to spread the "American way of life."

As in the past, Coca-Cola's continued growth also brought with it a strong focus on advertising. During the war, images of defense plant workers enjoying Coca-Cola filled the company's advertisements, and after the war, slogans such as "Sign of Good Taste" dominated the ads of the 1950s. During that decade, the Coca-Cola Company also added a new kind of advertising—television sponsorship. During the early years of television, companies would sponsor entire shows; rather than running commercials, they would weave advertisements for their products into the content of the programs. In

By the end of World War II, Coca-Cola had put down roots in European countries such as Great Britain

Drink
Coca-Cola

Delicious and Refreshing

Through the years, the Coca-Cola Company has come up with many memorable—and successful—slogans for its product, helping to lure customers and fuel sales. Here are some of the more famous ones:

1904 Delicious and Refreshing

1905 Coca-Cola Revives and Sustains

1911 Enjoy a Glass of Liquid Laughter

1917 Three Million a Day

1927 Around the Corner from Everywhere

1929 The Pause That Refreshes

1936 It's the Refreshing Thing to Do

1942 The Only Thing Like Coca-Cola Is Coca-Cola Itself

1944 Global High Sign

1952 What You Want Is a Coke

1963 Things Go Better with Coke

1969 It's the Real Thing

1979 Have a Coke and a Smile

1982 Coke Is It!

1988 You Can't Beat the Feeling

1990 Can't Beat the Real Thing

1993 Always Coca-Cola

2000 Coca-Cola. Enjoy!

2001 Life Tastes Good

2003 Coca-Cola ... Real

2006 The Coke Side of Life

1950, Coca-Cola sponsored its first television show, The Edgar Bergen and Charlie McCarthy Show, and it later sponsored the musical variety show *Coke Time* with Eddie Fisher. As sponsorship of entire shows eventually gave way to commercials, Coca-Cola began to air ads featuring celebrities such as singers Connie Francis and Anita Bryant.

Despite its success following World War II, Coca-Cola soon found itself entangled in another kind of war: the cola wars. Although Pepsi-Cola had been invented around the same time as Coca-Cola, the company had rarely been able to compete with Coke (although during the 1930s Pepsi had done well by offering a 12-ounce, or 355 ml, bottle for the same price as Coca-Cola's 6.5-ounce, or 192 ml, bottle).

"You can run from it, but you can't hide. Sooner or later, no matter how far you think you've ventured from the comforts and conveniences of the modern world, Coke will find you."

New York Times
Editorial, 1991

Coca-Cola spread rapidly after the mid-1900s, even into impoverished countries such as Kenya

In 1949, a former Coca-Cola executive assumed leadership at Pepsi, which soon began to emerge as a real Coke competitor.

By adding new bottle sizes and embarking on a huge advertising campaign, Pepsi was able to increase its sales by more than 100 percent between 1950 and 1955, causing great alarm among the Coca-Cola Company's leadership. In response, Coca-Cola created two new bottle sizes, the 10-ounce (295 ml) king-size and 26-ounce (770 ml) family-size bottles. The larger bottles were an instant hit, and Coke also increased the size of its drinks at soda fountains. Despite these steps, by the end of the 1950s, Pepsi-Cola had gained more than a third of the U.S. cola market.

With the cola wars in full swing, Robert Woodruff announced in 1955 that he was retiring, having reached the company's mandatory retirement age of 65. Although former newspaper publisher Bill Robinson took over as the company's president, Woodruff remained on the board of directors and served as chairman of the finance committee, where he continued to wield considerable power. In fact, after his retirement, Woodruff moved into an even bigger office in the company's Atlanta headquarters building, where he continued to go every day until he was in his 80s.

4

Introducing Something New

Until 1960, the Coca-Cola Company sold only one product: Coca-Cola. But that year, the company decided to expand its drink offerings by adding *Fanta*, a line of fruit-flavored soft drinks that had been sold by Coke bottlers in other countries for many years, to its beverage list.

Also in 1960, the Coca-Cola Company acquired the Minute Maid Corporation and added frozen juice concentrates to its lineup. The next year, the company introduced the citrus-flavored soft drink Sprite, and in 1963, it brought out its first low-calorie soft drink, called TAB.

While Coca-Cola was introducing its new drinks, Pepsi was introducing a new advertising campaign. With its "Pepsi Generation" ads, Coke's rival tried to convince consumers that Coca-Cola was drunk only by the aging World War II generation and that Pepsi was the drink of the young, hip new generation. In response, Coca-Cola came out with the "Things Go Better with Coke" ad campaign, which included radio and television spots featuring different popular music groups, such as the Supremes, singing a catchy jingle. At a cost of $53 million, this campaign made Coca-Cola the most heavily advertised product in the U.S. and helped to keep it ahead of Pepsi in the cola wars at home, although Pepsi often overtook Coke overseas.

The 1970s saw more innovative ads from Coca-Cola. In 1971, during the Vietnam War, the company released a commercial showing young people from across the globe joining together to sing the uplifting song "I'd Like to Buy the World a Coke." A non-Coke version of the song (titled "I'd Like to Teach the World to Sing") soon became a hit. Another popular commercial of the 1970s featured a young boy offering a Coke to Pittsburgh Steelers star "Mean" Joe Greene, causing the burly football player to smile and toss the boy his jersey.

With Coca-Cola's ads doing so well, Pepsi took a dramatic step in 1975 and introduced the "Pepsi Challenge," in which the company pitted Pepsi and Coke directly against each other. In a series of blind taste tests, people who reported that they were loyal Coke drinkers repeatedly chose Pepsi over Coke, with the results being aired in Pepsi's television commercials.

As the Pepsi Challenge continued, the Coca-Cola Company promoted Roberto Goizueta,

Pepsi-Cola grew from something of an imitator to a serious Coca-Cola rival in the 1960s and '70s who had begun working for Coke in Havana, Cuba, in 1954, to the position of chief executive to replace Paul Austin, who had served in the position since the 1960s. Goizueta then presided over a series of changes at the company. The first change was the 1982 introduction of Diet Coke (known as Coca-Cola Light in some countries), marking the first extension of the Coca-Cola brand. The new drink was immensely popular, and within two years, it had become the world's best-selling low-calorie soft drink. That same year, Goizueta announced that the company had acquired Columbia Pictures, a film and television production company, for $750 million. Although many scoffed at the purchase of a company in an unrelated industry,

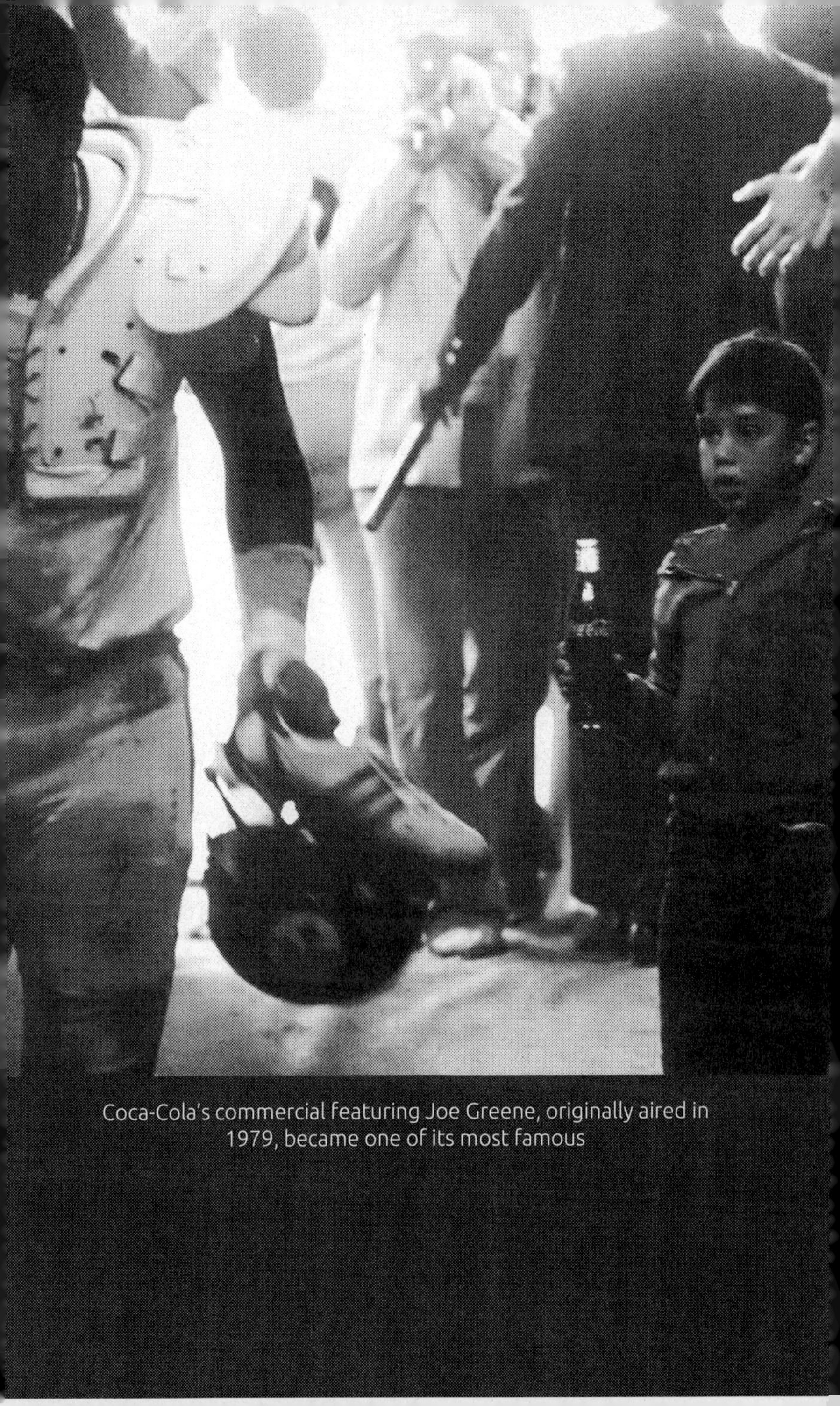

Coca-Cola's commercial featuring Joe Greene, originally aired in 1979, became one of its most famous

Columbia Pictures proved profitable to Coke, and when the company sold it in 1989, it was at a profit of more than $1 billion.

Neither the introduction of Diet Coke nor the purchase of Columbia Pictures would make as many headlines as Goizueta's other major change, however. In 1985, worried by the results of the Pepsi Challenge, the Coca-Cola Company decided to introduce a new formula for Coca-Cola. Calling their smoother, sweeter formula "New Coke," the company announced in April 1985, "The best has been made even better." Because blind taste tests had shown that 61 percent of people preferred new Coke over the original, company leaders were sure their new product would be a success. They were wrong.

What the blind taste tests couldn't show was people's loyalty to the original Coca-Cola. As soon as the new product was announced, the company began to receive calls and letters from angry consumers demanding that the original Coca-Cola be returned to store shelves. By May,

"An ice-cold Coke is … a simple pleasure, nothing fancy, offered not to solve the world's problems but to give … a simple moment of satisfaction and refreshment."

Don Keough,
Former President and Chief Operating Officer of the Coca-cola Company

Since the 1985 failure of New Coke, Coca-Cola's original formula has carried the "classic" label

Guarding the Formula

Since the early days of Coca-Cola, the beverage's "secret formula" has been a carefully guarded secret. In addition to sugar, caramel, caffeine, phosphoric acid, coca and cola extracts, and glycerin, the syrup for Coca-Cola contains a secret combination of flavorings and plant extracts that the company mysteriously refers to as Merchandise 7X. The full recipe for the formula is kept in a high-security safe-deposit box in the SunTrust Bank in Atlanta, and legend has it that the box can only be opened if the company's full board of directors votes to open it. In addition, only two senior officials at the company are allowed to know the formula at once, and those two officials are reportedly kept from ever traveling on the same airplane. The high level of secrecy surrounding the formula has only served to heighten the public's interest in it—yet another effective marketing tool employed by the Coca-Cola Company.

the company was fielding 8,000 calls a day. People began to stockpile supplies of old Coke, and some even poured bottles and cans of New Coke into storm drains in protest. A New York newspaper declared the new beverage "smoother, sweeter, and a threat to a way of life."

In response to the public outcry, Goizueta announced in July that the Coca-Cola Company would reintroduce Coke Classic, telling the American people, "We have heard you." The company's president, Don Keough, said, "The simple fact is that all the time and money and skill poured into consumer research on the new Coca-Cola could not measure or reveal the deep and abiding emotional attachment to original Coca-Cola felt by so many people.... The passion for original Coca-Cola—and that is the word for it: passion—was something that caught us by surprise.... It is a wonderful American mystery, a lovely American enigma, and you cannot measure it any more than you can measure love, pride, or patriotism."

The day that the change was announced,

Coca-Cola received 18,000 calls, this time from grateful consumers. In the following weeks, sales of Coke Classic surged, and by 1986, it had again overtaken Pepsi, which had briefly jumped ahead after the release of New Coke.

5
Refreshing the World

Fortunately for the Coca-Cola Company, the problems with New Coke didn't seem to hurt the company's image around the world. In 1988, three independent surveys found that Coca-Cola was the world's best-known and most admired trademark. A similar survey in 1990 showed that Coke was the most successful brand name in the world.

In order to showcase its success, in 1990, the company opened the World of Coca-Cola museum in Atlanta, which quickly began to attract Coke aficionados. Later in the 1990s, Coca-Cola collectors—who clamor after anything marked with the Coca-Cola logo—flooded new Coca-Cola stores in New York and Las Vegas, where they could purchase everything from vintage Coke postcards to neon Coca-Cola signs.

Throughout the '90s, Coca-Cola introduced a number of new beverages such as POWERade sports drinks, Fruitopia juices, Planet Java cold coffee drinks, and the caffeine-packed Surge citrus soft drink. By the end of the decade, Coca-Cola was selling more than one billion drinks a day, many of them in foreign countries as far-flung as Angola, Afghanistan, China, and Mexico.

In 1997, Roberto Goizueta died of lung cancer, and within two years, Doug Ivester, who had taken over as chief executive, found himself facing a crisis. In June 1999, a number of students in Belgium were taken to the hospital, claiming that Coca-Cola had made them sick. Although there was no evidence that the drinks had caused the illness, Coca-Cola issued an apology and instituted a $250-million product recall. But the damage to the company's image was already done, and in 2000, Ivester was replaced by Douglas Daft, a high-ranking Coca-Cola executive.

One of Daft's first projects as CEO was to preside over a massive restructuring of the company, which involved laying off huge numbers of people—something that had rarely been done in company history. Ultimately, 6,000 people—about 3,300 in the U.S. and 2,700 overseas—at all levels of the company, from payroll to maintenance, lost their jobs in the corporate shakeup that was intended to make the company more profitable. Also in 2000, the company settled a racial discrimination lawsuit that involved more than 2,000 past and current black employees, who claimed that the company had long passed over black employees for promotion in favor of white employees, and that white employees routinely

Soda options, quite limited in the mid-1900s, exploded in the 1990s, with many new varieties introduced received higher pay than black employees. The company offered those involved in the suit $192.5 million and agreed to work toward new diversity goals.

Despite its turbulent start to the new millennium, Coca-Cola continued to introduce new products to its beverage lines. In 2001, Diet Coke with lemon was added, and in 2002, the company introduced Vanilla Coke. At the same time, sales of Coke's Dasani brand of bottled water, which had been introduced in 1999, began to take off.

After the successful launch of so many products, Daft retired in 2004 and was replaced by E. Neville Isdell, a former Coke executive, who came out of retirement to take the position. Under Isdell, the company

A 2000 racial discrimination lawsuit against Coca-Cola stirred up unhappy memories of past prejudice

Enjoy!

The World Drinks Coke

One of the ways the Coca-Cola Company can tell how popular it is in a certain country is by looking at that country's per capita consumption. Per capita consumption refers to how many eight-ounce (237 ml) servings of Coca-Cola products are consumed by each person in a country in a year (this is found by dividing the number of Coca-Cola products sold by the population of the country). In 2005, per capita consumption of Coca-Cola products ranged from a low of one Coca-Cola product per person per year in Bangladesh to a high of 533 Coca-Cola products per person per year in Mexico. Here's a look at how some other countries compared:

Country	*Annual Servings Per Person*
China	18
Egypt	28
Russia	49
Zimbabwe	95
France	113
Philippines	151
Brazil	156
Japan	175
Great Britain	199
South Africa	235
Canada	247
Australia	323
United States	431

has continued to introduce new products, and today, Coca-Cola offers nearly 2,400 different drinks around the world. In Chile, consumers can buy Bibo, a snack drink fortified with vitamins. In Australia, youngsters drink high-energy Burn. In Japan, Coca-Cola's Qoo drink is a best-selling juice brand. In the U.S., Enviga, a sparkling green tea reported to help burn calories, was made available in 2007.

With so many beverages being sold in so many countries, the Coca-Cola bottling system is today one of the largest production and distribution systems in the world. As of 2006, the company—including the bottling plants it owns—employed 70,000 people, 49,000 of them outside of the U.S. Independent bottlers employed thousands more. Just as in the past, the Coca-Cola Company today still supplies syrup to its bottling plants, which then mix it with sugar and water, carbonate it, bottle it, and ship it. In some countries, the method of shipping can be unique: In Indonesia, boats carry Coca-Cola between islands. In the

"Coke's peaceful near-conquest of the world is one of the remarkable phenomena of the age. It has put itself … always within an arm's length of desire."

Time Magazine Article, 1950

In recent years, Coca-Cola has unveiled new products, sometimes in partnership with other companies

Amazon, Coca-Cola is floated down the river. And in the Andes Mountains, the drink is often carried by pack animals.

As the Coca-Cola Company moves farther into the new millennium, its goal is to keep adding new beverages. "Expanding our beverage portfolio is an important strategic priority," said John Brock, president and chief executive officer (CEO) of Coca-Cola Enterprises, the company's largest bottler. Although the Coca-Cola Company will keep soft drinks at its core, in the future, it will also increasingly roll out new products such as vitamin water, energy drinks, and health beverages. There has even been talk of a new "beauty" drink called Lumaé, which could be released as early as 2008 in partnership with the cosmetic company L'Oréal. The tea-based drink would reportedly provide skin-care benefits to women.

With its focus on new drinks, the Coca-Cola Company has certainly come a long way from that day in 1886 when John Pemberton accidentally discovered Coke's formula. Now, chemists regularly (and intentionally) mix ingredients in search of new beverages. And with those beverages reaching 6 billion of the planet's 6.6 billion people, the Coca-Cola Company looks to be well on its way to refreshing the world.

Glossary

acquired purchased another company

allies nations or groups that are friendly toward one another or that fight together against common enemies in a war

brand the name of a product or manufacturer; a brand distinguishes a product from similar products made by other manufacturers

carbonated water water that has been made bubbly using carbon dioxide

cocaine a highly addictive drug made from the leaves of the coca plant

discrimination treating a person or group unfairly because of prejudice; racial discrimination occurs when people are treated unfairly based on their race

enigma something that is difficult to understand; a mystery

extracts concentrated substances that are extracted, or taken out of, their sources, such as plants or fruit

glycerin a thick, sweet liquid used in a number of products, including some soft drinks, antifreeze, and cosmetics

Great Depression a time from 1929 to 1939 when there was widespread unemployment in the U.S. and elsewhere in the world and a major decline in the production and sale of goods

market a geographic region or segment of the population to which companies try to sell goods; for example, the North American market, the youth market, or the world market

marketing advertising and promoting a product in order to increase sales

pharmacist a person who prepares and distributes medicines

phosphoric acid a syrupy acid used in soft drinks, fertilizers, and medicines

rationed limited; during times of shortage such as war, governments sometimes set limits on the amount of a product that can be purchased by an individual or company

sarsaparilla a carbonated drink flavored with the root bark of the sassafras tree and oil from a

European birch tree

shares the equal parts a company may be divided into; shareholders each own a certain number of shares, or percentage, of the company

slogans short, attention-grabbing phrases used in advertising

stock shared ownership in a company by many people who buy shares, or portions, of stock, hoping the company will make a profit and the stock value will increase

tonic a mixture designed to refresh and restore people's energy

trademarked registered as belonging legally and exclusively to one company

Selected Bibliography

Allen, Frederick. Secret Formula: How Brilliant Marketing and Relentless Salesmanship Made Coca-Cola the Best-Known Product in the World. New York: HarperBusiness, 1994.

Bell, Lonnie. The Story of Coca-Cola. Mankato, Minn.: Smart Apple Media, 2004.

Gould, William. VGM's Business Portraits: Coca-Cola. Lincolnwood, Ill.: VGM Career Horizons, 1995.

Hays, Constance. The Real Thing: Truth and Power at the Coca-Cola Company. New York: Random House, 2004.

Pendergrast, Mark. For God, Country & Coca-Cola. New York: Basic Books, 2000.

Watters, Pat. Coca-Cola: An Illustrated History. Garden City, N.Y.: Doubleday & Company, 1978.

Young-Witzel, Gyvel, and Michael Karl Witzel. The Sparkling Story of Coca-Cola. Stillwater, Minn.: Voyageur Press, 2002.

Index

JAICO PUBLISHING HOUSE

Elevate Your Life. Transform Your World.

ESTABLISHED IN 1946, Jaico Publishing House is home to world-transforming authors such as Sri Sri Paramahansa Yogananda, Osho, The Dalai Lama, Sri Sri Ravi Shankar, Sadhguru, Robin Sharma, Deepak Chopra, Jack Canfield, Eknath Easwaran, Devdutt Pattanaik, Khushwant Singh, John Maxwell, Brian Tracy and Stephen Hawking.

Our late founder Mr. Jaman Shah first established Jaico as a book distribution company. Sensing that independence was around the corner, he aptly named his company Jaico ('Jai' means victory in Hindi). In order to service the significant demand for affordable books in a developing nation, Mr. Shah initiated Jaico's own publications. Jaico was India's first publisher of paperback books in the English language.

While self-help, religion and philosophy, mind/body/spirit, and business titles form the cornerstone of our non-fiction list, we publish an exciting range of travel, current affairs, biography, and popular science books as well. Our renewed focus on popular fiction is evident in our new titles by a host of fresh young talent from India and abroad. Jaico's recently established Translations Division translates selected English content into nine regional languages.

In addition to being a publisher and distributor of its own titles, Jaico is a major national distributor of books of leading international and Indian publishers. With its headquarters in Mumbai, Jaico has branches and sales offices in Ahmedabad, Bangalore, Bhopal, Chennai, Delhi, Hyderabad, Kolkata and Lucknow.

SINCE 1946